Designed by Flowerpot Press
www.FlowerpotPress.com
CHC-0909-0619
Made in China/Fabriqué en Chine
Copyright © 2025 Flowerpot Press,
a Division of Flowerpot Children's Press, Inc., Oakville, ON, Canada
and Kamalu LLC, Franklin, TN, U.S.A. All rights reserved. Can you find
the flowerpot? No part of this publication may be reproduced, stored
in a retrieval system or transmitted, in any form or by any means,
electronic, mechanical, photocopying, recording, optical scan, or
otherwise, without the prior written permission of the copyright holder.

WHY DO OKAPIS Look So Funny?

A BOOK ABOUT RAINFOREST ANIMALS

Written by Jack Beard Illustrated by Jayri Gómez

Have you ever wondered WHY animals in the rainforest do the things they do?

Rainforests are kingdoms of trees with their branches reaching as high as the sky. Hidden under the canopy of the rainforest are countless amazing animals. Each one has special traits to help them thrive in these jungle playgrounds.

gorilla

flower

frog

snake

How many yellow flowers do you see?

Why do brown-throated three-toed sloths move so slowly?

Give this slow sloth and his snail friend names!

snail

Are sloths just plain lazy and enjoy taking lots of naps?

Well, sort of. Brown-throated three-toed sloths only eat leaves which are not very filling and do not provide a lot of energy. Sloths have learned to conserve the little energy they do have by moving slowly and taking lots of naps!

Some sloths have two toes on each foot and some have three! How many toes do you have?

sloth

Why do capybaras like to swim?

Capybaras hang out in groups by riverbanks and like to wade into the water to cool off. They also swim to escape predators, like green anacondas or jaguars!

Why do mountain gorillas live in groups?
Is it so they can take awesome group selfies?

gorilla

Mountain gorillas like to live in groups because they are social butterflies, well...social apes. They communicate using body language and noises. Their faces are also very expressive and convey feelings and needs to each other.

leaf

tree

Gorillas live with their families. Who is in your family?

Why do Draco lizards have flat bodies?

Draco lizard

frog

Is it so they can disguise themselves as leaves?

tree

cloud

How many Draco lizards are hiding in the trees?

Draco lizards have flat bodies so they can glide! These lizards are also called flying dragons because their bodies have a wing-like shape that allows them to leap and glide from tree to tree.

canopy

tree trunk

Their unique look helps them hide from predators. Okapis live among the tree trunks in the rainforest, where their brown bodies and white stripes look like sunlight filtering through the trees.

Why do scarlet macaws have such colorful feathers?

Scarlet macaws have colorful feathers to help them hide in the rainforest! Their bright feathers confuse and distract potential predators.

tree

Their feathers also help scarlet macaws attract a potential mate. The brighter the colors, the better their chance of finding love.

cloud

leaf

Can you find the hidden sloth in the tree?

WHAT ELSE CAN RAINFOREST ANIMALS DO?

There is so much to learn about animals in the rainforest. Read more about each one here!

JAGUAR

Jaguars are the largest cats in North America and the third largest in the world!

Jaguars can roar like lions.

The black spots on a jaguar's body are called rosettes.

MOUNTAIN GORILLA

Mountain gorillas share 98% of their DNA with humans!

A gorilla's noseprint is unique to each gorilla.

Older male gorillas are called silverbacks because of a silver patch of hair that begins to grow as they age.

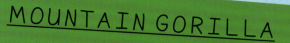

GREEN ANACONDA

Green anacondas can weigh up to 200 pounds (91 kg)!

Green anacondas can also swim.

SCARLET MACAW

Scarlet macaws bond with each other for life!

The scarlet macaw is the national bird of Honduras.

Scarlet macaws have strong beaks that can easily crack open nuts and seeds.

BLUE MORPHOS

Blue morphos are one of the largest butterflies in the world!

Only male blue morphos are blue.

BROWN-THROATED THREE-TOED SLOTH

Sloths move so slowly that algae grows on their fur!

Sloths sleep up to 20 hours a day.

Sloths have two or three curved claws on each of their feet that allow them to hang upside down from trees.

Draco lizard

Draco lizards spend almost all their time in trees and rarely go to the ground.

Draco lizards mostly eat ants and termites.

Capybara

Capybaras are the world's largest rodents!

A capybara's teeth never stop growing.

Poison Dart Frog

Poison dart frogs can be yellow, green, blue, orange, red, or multicolored.

Poison dart frogs are poisonous because of the insects they eat.

Poison dart frogs are some of the most poisonous animals in the world!

Okapi

Okapis are also called forest giraffes.

Okapis have four stomachs!

Okapis eat up to 65 pounds (29 kg) of food a day.